HINDUISM

Dilip Kadodwala

Thomson Learning
New York

Words appearing in *italic* in the text have not fallen into common English usage. The publishers have followed Merriam Webster's Collegiate Dictionary (Tenth Edition) for spelling and usage.

First published in the United States in 1995 by
Thomson Learning
New York, NY

Published simultaneously in Great Britain by Wayland (Publishers) Ltd.

U.S. copyright © 1995 Thomson Learning

U.K. copyright © 1995 Wayland Publishers Ltd.

Library of Congress Cataloging-in-Publication Data
Kadodwala, Dilip.
Hinduism / Dilip Kadodwala.
        p.   cm.—(World religions)
   Includes bibliographical references and index.
   Summary: An overview of the Hindu religion, including its history, scriptures, ceremonies, and customs.
   ISBN 1-56847-377-X (hc)
   1. Hinduism—Juvenile literature.
[1. Hinduism.] I. Title. II. Series.
BL1203.K33   1995
294.5—dc20   95-14422

Printed in Italy

Cover: Ringing the bell to announce the start of worship..
Title page: Hindu pilgrims at Tirumala.
Contents page: The festival of Holi, *in the Hindu month of* Phalguna *(February/ March), is enjoyed especially by children, who spray people with water mixed with colored dyes.*

Acknowledgments

The author is grateful for the priestly support given by Shri Jagdishbhai Bhatt in writing this book. Thanks also to my parents, my wife, Vilash, and our sons Devan and Viren. This book is dedicated to them.

The author and publishers thank the following for their permission to reproduce photographs: Circa Photo Library: *cover* (John Smith), pp. 8, 10, 17 (top), 24, 25, 35; Robert Harding Picture Library: p. 9; Hutchison Library: p. 41 (Liba Taylor); Christine Osborne Pictures: pp. 6, 15 (top), 19, 22; TRIP: pp. 1 (F. Good), 3 (H. Rogers), 4 (top),(P. Emmett), 4 (bottom) (B. Peerless), 5 (P. Emmett), 7 (top), (B. Peerless), 7 (bottom) (R. Graham), 11 (Vitahalbai Collection, Dinodia Press Agency), 12 (B. Turner), 13 (P. Ranter), 15 (bottom), 17 (bottom) (H. Rogers), 18 (P.Emmett), 20 (H. Rogers), 21 (P. Emmett), 23 (F. Good), 26, 27 (H. Rogers), 29 (P. Emmett), 30 (top) (P. Emmett), 30 (bottom) (H. Rogers), 31 (H. Rogers), 32 (P. Emmett), 33 (P. Emmett), 34 (H. Rogers), 37 (B. Turner), 38, 39 (P. Emmett), 42 (P. Emmett), 43 (P. Emmett), 44 (H. Rogers), 45 (top) (H. Rogers), 45 (bottom) (H. Rogers).

Contents

INTRODUCTION

The variety of ideas within the Hindu religion is like the variety of tastes in a traditional Indian vegetarian meal.

What does it mean to be a Hindu? You might expect the answer to be that a Hindu believes in the teachings of the person who founded the Hindu religion. But this answer would be wrong. Hinduism has no one single founder. Nor did the religion begin at any specific point in history. Hinduism is one of the oldest religions in the world, and most Hindus would agree that it is best understood as a rich and varied way of life.

The word "Hindu" comes from the name of a river in northern India. About 3,500 years ago, people called Aryans invaded the northwestern part of India, and they called the river the Indus. At first, the word "Hindu" was used to mean the people who lived beyond the Indus. Today the Hindu religion is still closely connected with India, where the great majority of Hindus live.

"Hinduism" is a more modern word, first used by Europeans in the early nineteenth century. Hindus themselves do not always recognize or use that word to describe their religion. They prefer dharma or Sanatan dharma, which means "the eternal religion." To be a Hindu means to be born into a tradition and a way of life and to share certain beliefs and practices.

The gateway towers of the Meenakshi temple in Madurai, southern India, stand about 160 feet high.

Imagine you are invited to a traditional Indian vegetarian meal. Usually it would be served as a *thali*, which means that the food is offered on one large circular stainless steel plate. On this plate would be a mix of spicy vegetables, rice, lentils, and fruits, each in a separate stainless steel bowl. You might also have some chapati or nan (types of bread) and a variety of chutneys. Now think of this *thali* as a symbol of Hinduism. Just as the food has a blend of ingredients and spices, so the religion has a variety of beliefs, and Hindus may approach them in varied ways.

These images of deities are on their way to be installed in a temple. It is a holy occasion, so the images are adorned with regal clothes and garlands of flowers.

Central to the religion (the circular plate) is the Hindu idea of God. Hindus describe God as "Brahma," which means the Supreme Being or Reality. Brahma has no form and is everywhere, in people, plants, and animals. "Atman" is the spirit of Brahma in humans.

It is not always easy to think of God as formless, so some Hindus use images of Brahma to help them worship. In this sense, Hindus believe that God can be worshiped in different forms. Hinduism therefore has thousands of gods and goddesses. Each represents some aspect of Brahma, and the vast number of them emphasizes the idea that Brahma is everywhere.

TRIMURTI

Hindus sometimes express their understanding of God as Trimurti: three images. These are Brahma, the Creator, Vishnu, the Preserver, and Siva, the Destroyer.

People believe that whenever there is an increase of evil in the world, the Supreme Being appears on earth to defeat evil. These appearances are called "avatars." For example, Vishnu is believed to have appeared as nine different avatars, including Krishna and Rama. He will appear in a tenth form, Kalkin.

DHARMA

Dharma has three meanings:

🕉 religion.

🕉 the form of things as they are in the universe and the power that maintains them. For example, the dharma of fire is to burn.

🕉 one's personal duty – to behave righteously and to fulfill one's obligations to family, society, and God.

At the entrance of the Mahalakshmi temple in Bombay, a worshiper has a tilak *mark put on his forehead before he goes inside to pray. Devout followers of Vishnu or Shiva have these markings, made with powders and ashes, to show their devotion to God.*

Two essential ingredients of the Hindu *thali* are the beliefs about "dharma" and "karma." Hindus say that each individual has his or her own dharma, meaning "duty". The idea of karma is that everything in the universe is subject to causes and effects. Individual good actions have good effects. If humans cause suffering to others, then they too will meet suffering.

This idea is linked to the Hindu belief that life is a cycle of birth, death, and rebirth, called "samsara." One's next existence depends on how far one fulfills one's dharma by living correctly and performing good actions—good karma.

Hindus aim finally to be released from the repeated cycle of birth, death, and rebirth. This release is called *moksha*. Three things are necessary to achieve it: good actions, an understanding that the spirit of God (Brahma) and the spirit in humans (atman) are linked and devotion to one's chosen god or goddess. Hindus sometimes refer to these three paths as karma yoga, *jnana* yoga, and bhakti yoga. They and the teachings of the Hindu scriptures are also essential ingredients of the Hindu *thali*.

THE HISTORY OF HINDUISM

The Hindu religion is as old as Indian civilization, which can be traced back almost five thousand years. A wide range of beliefs and practices have evolved over a very long period of time.

The Indus Valley, 3000-1700 B.C.E.

Archaeologists in the twentieth century made an exciting discovery of the remains of an ancient civilization in the Indus Valley. Some of these remains were found at Mohenjo-Daro and Harappa, in what is now called Pakistan. They showed that the people who lived here, from about 3000 to 1700 B.C.E. (Before the Common Era—see page 47), had a highly developed lifestyle.

This seal found at Mohenjo-Daro is evidence that bulls were important in the beliefs of the people of the Indus Valley.

The great bath discovered at Mohenjo-Daro is evidence that bathing was a part of religious practice for the Indus Valley people.

The archaeologists found figures and seals, which showed that people worshiped a mother goddess and a bull. Some of the figures are smoke-stained, perhaps because people kept a little lamp burning in front of them. It is also believed that the Indus Valley people practiced religious rituals linked with bathing. Such practices are continued by Hindus today.

Archaeologists also found examples of the swastika symbol in the Indus Valley. This is a cross with four arms of equal length, each one bent in the same direction. It is still an important symbol to Hindus today.

In Sanskrit the swastika sign means "bringing health." The arms represent paths to God. They are bent because the paths are difficult. The arms all come from a central point, and this shows how everything in the universe grows from a single source.

The symbol also represents the sun. This is why Hindus see the swastika as a sign of good fortune and protection against evil. It is used as a sign of God's blessing at a time of new beginnings. For example, the symbol is marked on a coconut, using *kum kum* (red paste) during a wedding ceremony.

This decorated arti *tray (see page 34) won first prize in a competition held at the festival of* Diwali.

The Aryan invasion

About 1500 B.C.E. a group of people called the Aryans invaded the northwestern part of India, the area of the Indus Valley. These Aryans were linked with the land of Persia (now called Iran). Over time, more Aryans came and fought with the people who were the original settlers. They eventually conquered these people and some were driven further south.

The Vedic period, 1500-600 B.C.E.

The Aryans worshiped deities (gods) associated with nature. Indra was "Lord of the Sky," Agni, the "Lord of Fire," and Varuna, "Lord of the Waters."

Their deities were male, but they adopted the worship of the mother goddess from the original inhabitants of the Indus Valley.

From about 1200 B.C.E. the Aryans composed hymns, which were remembered and passed on by word of mouth. These became the earliest Hindu scriptures, called the "Vedas." The period of the Aryans in India is therefore called the "Vedic period" and their religion is called the "Vedic religion."

The information we have about the religion comes from the Vedas. Instructions for fire sacrifices and the use of prayers also date from the Vedic period.

The Aryans organized their society according to occupation. One group was the priests or "Brahmins". Some people began to challenge the special power the priests had.

A Brahmin today reads from some sacred texts and explains their meanings to a group of worshipers.

Early Hinduism, 600 B.C.E.-200 C.E.

From about 600 B.C.E., criticism of the power of the priestly group or *varna* led to the development of other religions, Jainism and Buddhism. This had an effect on the Vedic religion.

Some people now worked out detailed rules for general behavior in life. The "Manusmriti" ("Laws of Manu") set out the duties of each of four *varnas*, or groups of society. These were the priests, rulers, merchants, and craftsmen. Teaching about the four stages of a person's life, with particular duties linked to each, also developed.

People paid less regard to the nature deities of the Vedic period and gave their devotion instead to the gods Vishnu and Shiva. Worship at home became more important than public worship, and the idea of showing love and devotion to a personal deity or god began to emerge.

Daily Hindu worship is often performed at home. Hindu homes have shrines especially for this purpose.

Also during this time the two epic scriptures, the "Mahabharata" and the "Ramayana," came into being.

The Puranic period, 300-1200 C.E.

Hindu practices as they are known today were fully developed between 300 and 1200 C.E.. This period is called "the Puranic period," after some texts called the "Puranas," which means "ancient stories." They contain some of the main Hindu myths and stories that influenced the religious beliefs and practices of ordinary people. A movement that encouraged all people to express devotion to a personal god began in southern India and gradually spread north. It is sometimes known as "bhakti," or devotionalism.

Also during the Puranic period, gifted religious thinkers developed complicated Hindu philosophy. Two of these thinkers were Shankara and Ramanuja. People today still study their ideas about questions such as "How are humans related to God?"

Modern Hinduism

During the nineteenth and twentieth centuries reform movements have emerged, and changes have been made to try to keep the main Hindu beliefs while adapting them to changing circumstances. The need to adapt is particularly great for Hindus who now live outside of India.

MAHATMA GANDHI (1869–1948)

In Gandhi's time, the British ruled India. Gandhi led a protest movement for Indian independence. He insisted that the protesters should not use any violence, and this idea was inspired by his belief, as a Hindu, that all life is sacred. Gandhi used the word *ahimsa*, which means more than just "nonviolence." For him, it also meant expressing love and humility.

Hindus gave Gandhi the title Mahatma, which means "great soul." This was because, through actions in his life, he showed how love could defeat evil. Even as he lay dying, after a man had shot him, Gandhi forgave his killer. His example has inspired people in the West who have wanted to bring about changes for the better in their societies. For instance, in the 1960s, Martin Luther King, Jr. led a movement, using nonviolent methods, to champion the rights of African Americans in the United States.

The modern period has also seen the rise of sects such as the Swaminarayan Hindu Mission and the International Society for Krishna Consciousness, popularly known as the Hare Krishna movement.

HARE KRISHNA

The Hare Krishna movement was founded by Bhaktivedanta Swami Prabhupada, who brought its ideas to the West in 1965. The ideas are based on the teachings of a saint called Chaitanya Mahaprabhu (1485-1533), who practiced his love for God by worshiping Krishna. People who belong to this movement are strict vegetarians. Sometimes groups of them walk through the streets, chanting:

Hare Krishna Hare Krishna Krishna Krishna Hare Hare
Hare Rama Hare Rama Rama Rama Hare Hare.

Hare means "God who forgives your wrongdoings."

Followers of the Hare Krishna movement chanting and dancing in the streets of Vladivostok, Russia

2
THE WORLD OF HINDUS

Of all religions, the Hindu religion has the third largest number of followers. It is closely associated with the land of India. In 1994, this vast country, which is larger than all of Western Europe, had a population of about 900 million. Around 83 percent of these people are Hindus. India has 16 main languages, which the government has officially recognized, and there are hundreds of regional dialects. It is hardly surprising that Hindu beliefs and practices vary from region to region.

The majority of Hindus live in India (and some in Pakistan), but there are also many in other countries. Their families have migrated from India over the past. Outside India and Pakistan, the greatest number of Hindus in one area are in East Africa. Large Hindu communities also exist in Nepal, Sri Lanka, South Africa, Bali in Indonesia, Surinam, and Fiji.

Celebrating the festival of Diwali at Udaipur, India. Diwali *or* Deepavali *means "a row of lights." Here the lights are floated on water.*

THE MEHTA FAMILY

Geeta Mehta and her family moved from Bombay to New York when she was ten. Five years later she says:

"We are vegetarians, because as Hindus we believe that all life is sacred and has to be respected. My father, who is a doctor, says that vegetarianism is good for health reasons too!

"In Bombay it was easier to live as Hindus. There was always a fresh supply of many different vegetables and fruit. When we went out to eat, we did not have to ask if the food had been cooked in vegetable oil. I am pleased that some fast-food places here use vegetable oil to make French fries.

"Here, we have a family shrine where we pray every morning and evening. We also go to a temple, especially for *Diwali*. My parents tell me stories from the Ramayana. I like watching it on video too. My father buys a monthly Hindu family newspaper called *Hinduism Today*. It is good because it reminds me that we are Hindus and that there are many like us all over the world."

In the past, some Hindus went to work in the West Indies, in places such as Trinidad and Tobago, and in Guyana. During the twentieth century, Hindus have also settled in Australia, Europe, Canada, and the United States. Many of them trace their roots to India and East Africa. Families still keep regular contact with relatives in these countries and often visit them.

Holy places

For a devout Hindu, the entire land of India is sacred. It is believed that God has four dwelling places, called *dhams*, at Badrinath in the north, Puri in the east, Rameshvaram in the south, and Dwarka in the west. These places have important temples dedicated to Vishnu and Siva. Some other temples in India are dedicated to the female aspect of God. One example is the Meenakshi temple in Madurai (see page 4).

A temple dedicated to Siva, in Kapalesawar, India.

At Puri the temple is dedicated to Jagannath, which is another name for Vishnu. During the annual festival of *Rathayatra*, a huge image of Jagannath is mounted on a giant chariot and pulled along the streets of Puri. The English word "juggernaut" comes from the name of this deity.

Mountains and rivers are the other major holy sites. Some Hindus call the Himalayas "the dwelling place of the gods." Many journey to the mountains, such as Abu, as a way of purifying their minds and bodies and as a way of experiencing God.

Crowds at the Rathayatra *festival*

Pilgrimage

Hindus from across India and other parts of the world make pilgrimages to holy places. They may undertake journeys to visit their gurus (religious and spiritual teachers), because they have made special vows, or as a way of offering thanks to God. Others see their pilgrimage as a way of gaining merit, or good karma.

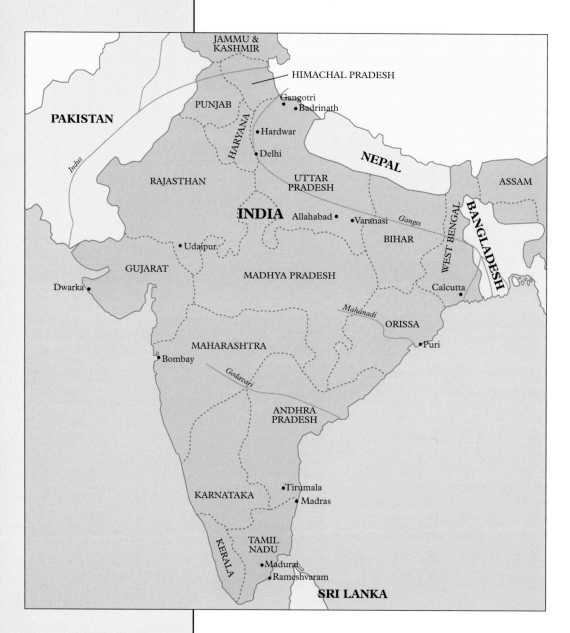

The holy city of Varanasi (Benares), on the banks of the Ganges, is especially important to Hindu pilgrims.

The Ganges River

Hindus call this river the "Ganga" and describe it as "the River of Heaven" because of the belief that it flowed in heaven before coming to earth. Pilgrims to the Himalayas climb to Gangotri, where the river first emerges from under a glacier.

A Hindu belief is that bathing in the Ganges washes away the bad karma of previous lives. Dawn is thought to be the best time for bathing, and at Varanasi, which is sometimes called "Kashi" (City of Light), Hindus from all backgrounds bathe and perform worship.

Hardwar and the city of Allahabad, often called Prayag, are other special places on the Ganges. At Prayag, the Ganges and Yamuna rivers meet. A colorful festival called the *kumbhamela* takes place here every 12 years. Millions of pilgrims attend.

The Ganges is often shown in art as flowing from Siva's hair and down through the Himalayas. This figure of Siva is from the door of the Siva temple in Mombasa, Kenya.

Dawn worship at Varanasi. Many devout Hindus also express a wish to die at Varanasi, or, at least, to have their ashes scattered on the Ganges there. They believe that Varanasi is the crossing place between heaven and earth. Therefore to die there is to be freed from the cycle of rebirth.

17

3

SHASTRAS

Most Hindu scriptures are in the ancient Indian language called Sanskrit. The Sanskrit word for scriptures is *shastras*. It means "texts that explain and guide the way people behave in life."

THE SCRIPTURES

Hindu scriptures, or *shastras*, have been divided into two groups. Some are called *shruti*, which means "heard" or "revealed" scriptures. This refers to wise men in ancient times who are believed to have heard God's word directly. The second group of scriptures is called *smriti*, which means "remembered." The scriptures were passed on orally for hundreds of years before they were written down.

The Vedas

The *shruti* texts include the four Vedas, which are some of the oldest Hindu scriptures. "Vedas" means "knowledge" or "wisdom." The first is the "Rig-veda," which contains hymns praising the gods and goddesses of the Aryan people.

The four Vedas were composed between 1200 and 1000 B.C.E. Priests memorized them and passed them on by word of mouth. It was not until about 1400 C.E. that they were first written down.

Public readings from the sacred texts are often given, especially during festivals

A PRAYER TO SAVITRI

The Rig-veda contains a prayer to Savitri, a sun god. Hindus recite this prayer every morning.

*Om bhur bhuvah svahah
tatsavitur varenyam
bhargo devasya dhimahi
dhiyo yo nah prachodayat*

This can be translated as:

"We meditate on the loving light of the god, Savitri. May his brilliance, like that of the sun, stimulate our thoughts."

The prayer is also known as the Gayatri mantra. Hindu children are encouraged to learn it by heart.

In some villages in India, a home shrine is outside but still within the boundary of the home.

ॐ भूर्भुवः स्वः तत्सवितुर्वरेण्यं भर्गो देवस्य धीमहि धियो यो नः प्रचोदयात्॥

The Gayatri mantra written in Sanskrit

The Upanishads

Also among the *shruti* texts are scriptures called the "Upanishads." Literally, the word means "near-down-sit." Imagine a group of young men sitting down near their older teachers, called gurus, deep in the forests of northern India, at the foot of the Himalayas. They would be discussing ideas about the nature of the universe and why humans were created. The beliefs that came out of these discussions, about Brahma, the Supreme Being, and atman, the human soul, were recorded in the Upanishads between 800 and 600 B.C.E..

There are 108 Upanishads. The shortest consists of only eighteen verses, of two or four lines.

Holy men called "sadhus" sometimes travel the length and breadth of India, visiting places regarded as especially holy. This sadhu is in Hardwar, a pilgrimage site in northern India.

THE BRIHADARANYAKA UPANISHAD

From the unreal
lead me to the real

From the darkness
lead me to light

From death
lead me to immortality.

These verses remind Hindus that, ultimately, only God is real. This does not mean that life on earth is not real, or that death is not real. But humans should not be fooled into thinking that life is all that there is and that there is nothing beyond. People who truly understand this achieve everlasting life. This text is sometimes read during a death ceremony.

The Mahabharata

The ideas and experiences of wise men recorded in the *shruti* texts were not easy for most Hindus to understand. Therefore, commentaries and stories were developed to convey the spiritual truths contained in the texts and to make sure these were not lost. The stories were often acted out in the many villages of India.

The first of the stories, or epics, is called the Mahabharata. It belongs to the *smriti* ("remembered") group of scriptures. The Mahabharata has 100,000 verses and includes the Bhagavad Gita, the "Song of the Lord."

The Bhagavad Gita

The Bhagavad Gita is the most respected of the Hindu scriptures. In it, Krishna, who is one of the avatars (forms) of Vishnu, the Preserver, reveals himself to his friend Arjun. He has come as God, in human form, to teach people how to overcome evil and how to lead dutiful lives.

The Bhagavad Gita deals with some of the more difficult ideas discussed in the Upanishads, but in a way that all Hindus can understand. In it, Krishna explains, for example, how humans can overcome the cycle of birth, death, and rebirth, particularly through loving devotion – bhakti – toward him. The Bhagavad Gita has been translated into many Indian languages and also into English.

Stories about the lives of gods and goddesses are often explained through dance and drama. This dancer is performing a story about Krishna.

21

DEVOTION TO KRISHNA

When a Hindu offers gifts to God, he or she may remember this verse from the Bhagavad Gita. In it, Krishna is saying that the size of the offering is not as important as the love that the Hindu has in his or her heart.

pattram pusham phalam toyam
yo me bhaktya prayacchati,
tad aham bhakty-upahrtam
asnami prayat'atmanah.

"Whoever offers to me a leaf,
a flower, a fruit, or water with
  devotion,
that offering of devotion, I will
  accept
from the pure of heart."

Krishna is often portrayed as blue and playing a flute. There are many stories of Krishna winning the hearts of girls who herded cows. This is another way of saying that God returns the love humans show for him.

The Ramayana

The second of the epic stories is called the Ramayana. It consists of 24,000 verses and tells the story of the great god Rama and his wife Sita, who is captured by an evil demon. After a series of adventures, she is finally rescued. The story stresses the importance of faithfulness, love, and truth and shows how good overcomes evil.

The Puranas

Other important scriptures are called the Puranas, which means "ancient stories." These also contain very long verses that relate Hindu myths. The stories encourage Hindus to live dutiful lives.

4

HOME AND FAMILY LIFE

Children born into a Hindu family begin to learn about their religion at home. There is much that they can learn about Hindu beliefs and practices simply by living in a family and in a Hindu community.

Family relationships

In India, people live mostly in extended families. Parents, children, grandparents, and often aunts and uncles all live together as part of one household. Grandparents play a large part in teaching the children about their religion.

In the West, Hindus do not always live in extended families. If they can, different branches of a family live close to one another so that the children can benefit from the wisdom passed on across generations.

Many Hindus mark new beginnings, such as moving to a new home, with religious ceremonies.

PUJA AT HOME

"When I wake up, I look at my hands. The fingers remind me of Lakshmi and the wrist reminds me of Saraswati. The palms remind me that God is ever-present in my life.

"After my bath, I perform *puja* with my mother. She washes the *murti* (statue image) of Siva and puts a small garland of flowers around it. She lights a ghee lamp and some incense, and then puts some *kum kum* paste on Siva's forehead, using the fourth finger of her right hand. We have pictures of other gods and goddesses too and their foreheads are marked with *kum kum*. We also offer them sweets and fruit.

"Next we do *arti*. My mother moves a ghee lamp clockwise in front of the *murti* and the pictures while we sing a prayer. We hold our hands over the lighted flame and then move them over our foreheads. This means we are receiving the blessings of Siva.

"My mother repeats the holy names of God, running her fingers through a *mala* of 108 wooden beads. Finally, we share the food we have offered to the gods, so that we feel blessed and ready to face the day ahead." (Usha, age 11, from Delhi, India)

Circling the arti *tray in front of a* murti.

Worship at home

Every home has a shrine where women in particular perform *puja* (worship) every day. Worship can be long or short and can involve all the members of a family, including men. It takes place in the morning and evening, although in the West some Hindu families choose to worship in the evening only, if the adults have to leave for work very early.

Washing murtis *with milk and water*

KATHA

"Three or four times a year we have a *katha*, a religious gathering, at home. Twenty to thirty people attend, so we clear the furniture from the shrine room and everyone sits on the floor. A Brahmin begins by performing *puja*. The sweet-smelling incense gives the feeling that God is present with us.

"After the *puja* the priest chooses a story from his books. He tells the story without really looking at the book, and explains the difficult parts – sometimes in English! The story is usually about people or families who have had experiences of God.

"One story I remember is about a man who lived a bad life, stealing and lying. Then, one day, he was passing through a village where a *katha* was taking place. He stopped to listen and this event changed his life completely. Stories like this are reminders to Hindus that God is everywhere. Treating all other people as if God is in them is another way of worshiping God.

"After the story, we sing *bhajans* (hymns) and finish by sharing the food (*prashad*) that the priest has offered to God."
(Bharat, age 12, from London)

Duties through life

Hindus see life as consisting of four stages – the *brahmacharya* (student) stage, the *grihastha* (householder) stage, the *vanaprastha* (retirement) stage, and the *saanyas* (renunciation) stage.

Hindus also have four aims in life – to do their duty (dharma), to make wealth (*artha*) to help others, to fulfill their ambitions (*kama*) but not to become attached to their success, and to gain release (*moksha*) from the cycle of rebirth.

Depending on which stage of life a person is in, one or some of these aims are seen as the most important.

For example, Hindus in the first, *brahmacharya* stage of life are encouraged to learn scriptures and to be educated so that they may earn a living. Children also learn to respect their elders as part of performing their duties.

In the villages of India especially, people make patterns from colored rice flour on their doorsteps. These patterns are a way of welcoming God to the home. During the festival of Diwali, *competitions for designing patterns are often held.*

At the *grihastha* stage, men and women are expected to marry and have children and to contribute to the well-being of the community and of society. Part of the duties of a householder is to care for family members, including the elderly. A householder should contribute to charities and help others by doing community work.

The *vanaprastha* stage begins at about the age of 50, when a person has probably fulfilled the desire to bring up a family and no longer needs to be as concerned about making money. The scriptures recommend that, at this stage, a person should begin to devote more time to spiritual matters. The person now goes more often to the *mandir* (temple) and to

satsangs (gatherings where scriptures, stories, and songs are recited), often held in Hindu homes.

At the *sannyas* stage, a person is supposed to give up all attachment to the material world and become a wandering monk. This gives the person time to concentrate on achieving *moksha*, final release from the cycle of birth, death, and rebirth.

The aims given for the four stages of life set out broadly what a Hindu should try to achieve during the course of a lifetime. In practice, people do not fit rigidly into this pattern. Not all Hindus become forest dwellers at the fourth stage of life, for example. For Hindus living in the West, it is more difficult to divide life into the four stages. Generally, however, the four stages give a framework within which Hindus can practice their religion and fulfill their duties.

A person who carries out all his or her religious and moral duties according to his age, *varna*, occupation, and financial means is said to be being true to his or her dharma.

Selling flowers outside a temple in Hardwar. Flowers are offered to God during worship. Also, in India, a way of greeting special guests and holy people is to place garlands of flowers around their necks.

VARNAS AND CASTES

The dividing of Indian society into groups goes back to ancient times. The Rig-veda describes four *varnas*: Brahmin (priest), Kshatriya (ruler), Vaishya (merchant), and Shudra (craftsman). Each group had particular duties. The idea was that if each group fulfilled its duties, society would work well.

Later, *varnas* became incorrectly mixed with castes, and this caused problems. Castes or *jatis* were smaller groups, often linked to occupations. People were not allowed to marry outside their group, and castes seen as lower ones were treated badly.

In modern India, the traditions of caste are less strictly observed.

Belonging to a group

Hindus everywhere attach importance to the group of society, called the *jati*, into which they are born. Originally, each *jati* was linked to an occupation and members of the *jati* all followed that occupation. Nowadays, people have more educational opportunities than in the past, and it is common to move to find work, because of this members of a *jati* can get jobs quite different from the traditional occupation of their group. This is especially the case in the West and in Indian cities. In the villages of India there has been less change. A person's *jati* can affect where he or she can live and with whom he or she can mix. It is still usual for Hindus, including those in the West, to marry someone from their own group.

BELONGING TO A JATI

"We belong to the *mochi* (shoemakers) *jati*. My grandfather was a shoemaker in Gujarat, India. He felt that education was very important and encouraged my father to study hard. Now my father is a pharmacist working in a London hospital and my grandfather is very proud of him.

"We have a hall we can use, which was bought by our jati association with money given by other mochis. I go to classes there on Saturday mornings to learn to read and write Gujarati. We speak that language at home. The jati association also holds dances and festival celebrations at the hall. I like meeting other mochi families, especially other children who were born in England. It feels good to belong!"

(Harish Chudsana, age 14, Birmingham, England)

5

COMMUNITY LIFE

Hindus come together at a *mandir* (temple) to perform *puja* (worship) and to keep strong links with other Hindus. In the West, Hindus also meet at the *mandir* to discuss community matters, and they hold events there to raise money to help others. Many *mandirs* have halls where weddings take place and rooms for classes, in which children learn languages and more about their religion.

Mandirs

There are thousands of *mandirs* in India. Some are huge, with beautiful and complicated designs inside and out. There are also tiny village and roadside shrines. This expresses again the idea that Brahma, the Supreme Being, is everywhere and is revealed in many forms.

A small mandir in India with an image of the deity Hanuman above the central door and one of Ganesh on the right.

Inside a mandir. *The alcove at the back is empty, waiting for the* murtis *(images, shown on page 5) to be installed.*

Hindus believe that a *mandir* is a house where a deity or deities live. Each *mandir* is dedicated to Vishnu, Siva, or Shakti, the mother goddess. However, some temples house all three deities plus others, such as Ganesh and Hanuman. The main shrine in the temple has the image or *murti* of the deity to whom the temple is dedicated. Surrounding shrines hold the *murtis* of the other deities.

Particular animals are associated with some deities. Images of these, and symbols and objects connected with the deities, may also be found in the temple.

In the West a *mandir* is usually a converted house or church. However, temples have been built in some major cities where Hindu communities have become more settled.

A well-known image of Siva is in the form of a dancer called Natraja. The circle of flames represents the destruction and recreation of the universe.

Gods and goddesses

All the gods and goddesses of Hinduism are images of different aspects of Brahma, the one Supreme Being who has no form and is everywhere.

Most Hindus worship Vishnu, the Preserver, or Siva, the Destroyer. It is possible to worship both of these deities, even though they seem contradictory. They represent opposite forces, which balance each other in life. Although Siva is the Destroyer, he also has a creative aspect. He destroys and then re-creates the world. Siva's creative side reveals itself as energy, which takes shape as the goddess Kali or the goddess Durga. The energy is both creative and destructive, so the goddesses are both gentle and terrible.

Both Vishnu and Siva appear in many forms. Siva is sometimes pictured as a householder who has a wife, the goddess Parvati. Their son is called Ganesh and their daughters are Lakshmi, the goddess of wealth and prosperity, and Saraswati, the goddess of knowledge and learning.

Some deities are portrayed with multiple faces and arms. Brahma, the creator of the universe, has four faces so that he can look in every direction at once. This is also a way of saying that God is everywhere. Brahma's four arms symbolize the points of the compass.

Most Hindu gods and goddesses have animals as their vehicles. The animals also represent some quality of the deity. A powerful bull called Nandi is usually linked with Siva.

ANIMALS

Animals are believed to support the powers of the deities. Siva's animal is a bull called Nandi. The goddess Parvati rides a tiger. Pictures like this show the deities' mastery over powerful animals. Siva also wears a five-headed cobra, usually over his head.

Brahma's hands carry symbolic objects: a water jug, as water is the source of life; a spoon, symbolizing offerings made during worship; prayer beads, a symbol of time; and a lotus flower, representing the universe, humanity, and purity. Brahma's vehicle is a goose, which symbolizes wisdom.

Vishnu is shown with sky-blue skin. Like the sky, he is everywhere and everlasting. In his four hands he carries a lotus, a conch shell, a club, and a wheel called chakra. The chakra symbolizes the circle of time, creation, and death.

Worship

Hindus perform daily worship at home, so they are not expected to go to the *mandir* every day. *Puja* in the *mandir* takes place in the evening, although in some temples in India it takes place throughout the day. Every *mandir* has at least one person, called a *pujari*, who leads the worship. A Hindu priest who conducts worship and also acts as a religious adviser has the title of pandit.

Ganesh is a popular Hindu deity. His pot belly symbolizes the universe and his elephant head represents his power to remove obstacles.

Worship follows a similar pattern at home and in a *mandir*. Before starting *puja*, worshipers bathe. In India, Hindus living near the Ganges immerse themselves in the river.

In the *mandir*, the *pujari* washes the *murtis* in water or milk. The images of the deities are treated as if they were honored guests or royalty. Next, the *pujari* anoints the *murtis* with sandalwood, turmeric, or *kum kum*. A *pujari* has a *tilak* mark on his forehead, made with these powders, and he makes a similar *tilak* mark on the *murtis*. He dresses the *murtis* in red and gold clothes and puts garlands of flowers on them. He offers food to them, usually in the form of fruit, and

uses incense to purify and sweeten the air around them.

The worshipers do not see these preparations being made. The *pujari* performs all these rituals behind curtains. As he prepares, he chants short sacred texts called mantras and recites prayers, in Sanskrit. Finally, before the curtains are drawn back so that the deities can receive the worshipers' praise, the *pujari* lights the *arti* lamp or *diva*. When the curtains are drawn back, the worshipers can "see" and, it is believed, are "seen" by God. Hindus call this special moment *darshan*.

A conch shell is often linked with Vishnu and his avatar Krishna, because it symbolizes a demon that Krishna destroyed. It reminds Krishna's devotees to destroy evil and ignorance in their lives. In a *mandir*, the conch shell is blown to announce the start of worship.

A bell is used for a similar purpose. The bell's ringing reminds the worshiper that he or she must try to concentrate on *puja* and drive away bad thoughts.

Lakshmi, the goddess of prosperity and good fortune, is often shown standing on a lotus flower. The goddess Saraswati is sometimes pictured riding a white goose.

33

Arti is the offering of five lighted lamps, made by dipping cotton wicks in clarified butter called ghee. The number five represents the five elements of nature essential for human survival – water, fire, earth (including its products, such as fruit and flowers), air, and space. The number five represents the five human senses. The idea is that people use all five senses in worship and so express their love, bhakti, for God with their whole being.

An arti *lamp in the form of the om symbol.*

Then the *pujari* performs the *arti* ceremony. On behalf of the worshipers he places the five lamps in a steel tray and moves the tray in a circle in front of the image of the main deity. This circling is done clockwise, from the top to the bottom of the *murti*. The tray is then moved from left to right to left again to make another circle. While this is happening, the worshipers sing a special hymn and chant a prayer. The singing is accompanied by music played on a harmonium, drums, and cymbals. It ends with the worshipers' request to God: "Bless me with ever-increasing faith, divine love, and spirit of service."

The *pujari* then circles the *arti* tray to the other three sides of the *mandir.* He sprinkles water, held in a conch shell, over the worshipers as a way of sharing God's blessings. As the worshipers sit down, they continue to share the blessings by passing the *arti* tray around. They put an offering of money in the tray and pass their hands over the lamps and then over their eyes as a sign of receiving God's blessings. As the worshipers leave the *mandir,* they take food blessed by God. This *prashad* is made of nuts, fruit, and sweets.

The sacred om

An important Hindu symbol is the sacred syllable om, sometimes spelled as AUM. This represents the sound of God. It is also the origin of all sound. The three letters are linked with Brahma, Vishnu, and Siva – with birth, life, and death. This syllable is recited at the beginning and ending of prayers and when *bhajans* (hymns) or mantras (holy chants) are sung. The Mandukya Upanishad opens with these words: "Everything is AUM. The past, present, and the future and that which is outside time. Everything is AUM."

6

A HINDU LIFETIME

The most important aim in life for a Hindu is to achieve release (*moksha*) from the cycle of birth, death, and rebirth. To achieve *moksha*, a Hindu has to develop self-control and must not become attached to successes in his or her present life. By following the requirements of dharma a person can gain good merits and so stand a better chance of achieving *moksha*.

The scriptures recommend sixteen steps to help achieve the goal of *moksha*. These steps are called *samskars*, or life-cycle rituals or sacraments. Eleven of the rituals are performed during the first stage of life. They begin even before a baby is born. The sixteenth step takes place after a person has died.

An expectant Hindu mother reciting prayers for a healthy child

Birth

Some ceremonies are performed to ensure the well-being of the mother-to-be and her baby during pregnancy. Customs vary depending on the *jati* people belong to and on where they live. A ceremony that is common to everyone occurs halfway through or toward the end of pregnancy. People recite prayers for a healthy child. The ceremony is followed by a feast for family members.

Some boys' names linked to names of gods are Mahesh, Jagdish, and Niranjan.

Girls' first names include Avni, which means "earth," Padma, which is the name for the lotus flower, and Usha, meaning "dawn." The girls' names Parvati, Savita, and Ansuya are linked to names of goddesses.

Another ceremony is performed on the day of a baby's birth. In the presence of a Hindu priest, the father takes a gold ornament, such as a ring, dips it in a mixture of ghee and honey, and holds it to the baby's lips. The father or the priest recites: "May your life be as precious as gold. This will depend on your good thoughts, speech, deeds, and behavior."

The father or priest then whispers in the baby's right ear: "May God the creator of all things grant you firm wisdom. Knowledge and wisdom are the source of power and long life." Family members, particularly grandparents, then bless the baby.

Naming a baby

The step of naming a child is taken on the twelfth day after birth. After a baby is born, the family asks a priest about names. The priest consults an almanac (a book giving information about each day in the year) and produces some syllables that can be used in the name. Some names have meanings associated with gods and goddesses or with the powers of nature.

In Gujarati Hindu families, the father's sister is given the honor of choosing the name.

The first outing

The baby is not taken outdoors for the first five weeks of his or her life. The scriptures recommend that the fourth month after birth is the ideal time for taking a baby outside for the first time. However, especially in the West, Hindu families find this recommendation difficult to follow. In ancient times, it was perhaps a way of ensuring that the child was protected from extreme weather conditions and from infectious diseases. On the baby's first outing, he or she is taken to a *mandir* to be blessed by God.

The first haircut

The eighth step, the first haircut or *mundan*, applies to male children, although a hair-cutting ceremony for girls is not unheard of. The ceremony takes place at the age of one, or before the age of three or five. Until then, the hair is left uncut.

Hindus believe that the haircutting ceremony is a way of making sure that the karma of the child's previous life, as well as impurities collected in the process of being born, are washed away. Some Hindu families, especially in India, put the hair in flowing water, for example in the Ganges. At the haircutting ceremony the parents express their wish that the child will be blessed with a fresh start in this new life.

After a haircutting ceremony

ASHOK'S HAIR-SHAVING

Ashok had his hair-shaving ceremony at the age of five. It would have been sooner, but it had to be delayed because his aunt died. A Hindu belief is that a year must go by after a death in the family, before a ceremony such as the first hair-cut is held. Ashok had had to put up with being mistaken for a girl!

A Hindu priest was invited to perform a sacred fire ritual before the haircutting. Afterward, Ashok sat, rather fidgety, in his father's lap and the barber began to shave off all Ashok's hair. He used an electric shaver, which probably made the experience less unsettling than if he had used a razor, as in ancient times.

A little cool yogurt was put on Ashok's bare head. Hindus regard yogurt as a pure substance, because it is made from milk. Then Ashok was bathed and his head was covered with a turban-shaped hat.

The sacred thread ceremony

The tenth of the sixteen steps is the sacred thread ceremony, or *upanayana*. It is for boys who belong to the first three varnas. The scriptures recommend that for boys in the Brahmin varna the ceremony take place in their eighth year; for boys in the Kshatriya varna, in their eleventh year; and for those in the Vaishya varna, in their twelfth year. Not all Hindu families in these three varnas have this ceremony performed. Some may leave it until the men are in their early twenties. This ceremony is both religious and social. It is per-

When the ceremony is performed in the earlier years, it also marks the boy's coming of age. It marks a time when a boy has begun to understand the meaning of belonging to a Hindu community. It also marks the beginning of his formal religious education.

formed in front of family and friends. A priest conducts a sacred fire ritual, called *homa*, and then places a loop of white cotton thread, made from three strands, over the boy's left shoulder so that it hangs diagonally across his chest and under his right arm. The boy makes a vow to remain celibate until marriage and to fulfill his duties toward God, his parents, and his religious teacher. To celebrate, after the ceremony there is a meal, and the boy receives presents.

A Hindu wedding

A Hindu sees marriage as holy, as it is the twelfth of the sixteen steps. Marriage is not only a union between two partners, but also an alliance of two families. In the past, the choosing of partners was left entirely to parents. It was their duty to arrange a match, taking into account the caste and social positions and the future happiness of the proposed couple and their off-spring. Now young people are increasingly involved in choosing their own partners. These days a Hindu marriage is "guided" rather than arranged.

Once the choice is made, a priest looks up the partners' horoscopes to find a good time for the wedding. The bride's family arranges and pays for the use of a hall or *mandir* and provides a feast. Relatives may travel great distances to attend.

At the ceremony, the priest performs several rituals. Depending on the wishes of the families, a ceremony can last for up to six hours. The sacred fire, or *homa,* is important. It is lit in a square metal or brick structure called a *yajna-kund.* The priest invites the groom to drop ghee and grains (symbols of fertility) into the fire and, as he does so, the bride, seated on his left, touches him on the right shoulder with her right hand. They both walk around the fire, holding hands, and

the groom says: "Let us love and admire one another and protect each other. Let us see, hear, and live a hundred autumns."

They offer prayers for a long and happy life and for God's blessings for children. Some elements used during the ceremony, such as coconuts and rice, also represent fertility and the hope for healthy children.

A highlight of the wedding ceremony is when the couple takes seven steps. The bride follows the groom, who says to her as they walk:

Take the first step for food.

Take the second step for power.

Take the third step for prosperity.

Take the fourth step for happiness.

Take the fifth step for children.

Take the sixth step for the enjoyment of pleasures.

Take the seventh step for lifelong friendship.

Taking the seven steps

LIFE AFTER DEATH

It is written in the Bhagavad Gita:
"Just as a man casts out worn-out clothes and puts on new ones, so also the embodied Self casts out worn-out bodies and enters others that are new."

Hindus believe that where a human being is reborn and in what form depends on good and bad deeds gathered through life. Of course, the family and friends of the one who has died hope that she or he will not be reborn at all, but will achieve release from the cycle of rebirth.

Death and funerals

When someone dies, Hindus freely express their sorrow. Family, friends, and neighbors give support. Comfort is also found in Hindu beliefs about life after death.

Hindu bodies are cremated (burned), not buried. At the cremation, the last of the sixteen life-cycle rituals is performed.

In India it is usual for a funeral pyre to be built near a river. If the person who has died is a man, close male relatives bathe his body and dress him in new clothes. Female relatives do the same if the dead person is a woman. Wood, saffron, musk, sandalwood, and camphor are used to make the funeral pyre. The eldest son or a close male relative lights the fire. A priest recites mantras in Sanskrit. When the body is reduced to ashes, they and the few bones that remain are collected and cast into a river. This is preferably the Ganges, because it is regarded as holy.

In the West, a funeral ceremony takes place at a crematorium, without a funeral pyre. Prayers and mantras are recited as in India. If possible, the family scatters the ashes in running water. More and more families now send the ashes to India, where they are scattered over the Ganges. Others make a special journey to scatter the ashes there themselves.

After the funeral, in some families, it is customary to eat some simple but specially prepared food, such as rice. The belief is that, if many people eat this food, there is a greater chance that the dead person's soul will find peace.

Fourteen days after the funeral, the family holds a feast. After this, they have an annual ceremony as a way of remembering the person who died.

7

FESTIVALS

For Hindus, time is not linear, with a beginning and an end, but turns like a wheel. Time is cyclical, and it is divided into four ages called "yugas."

Hindu months are based on the waxing and waning of the moon. Each month of thirty days has a light fortnight leading up to the full moon and a dark fortnight ending with the new moon. Because the calendar is lunar, the Hindu year is shorter than a year on the Western calendar. Festivals fall at changing times in the Western year and Hindus in the West use a calendar called a *pattra* to keep track of festival dates.

Twelve lunar months make a Hindu year. However, each year is counted as only one day in a gods' year. There are 360 Hindu years in one gods' year, and 12,000 gods' years make up a cycle of four ages, or yugas.

We are now in the worst age, the fourth yuga of the cycle, which began this time with a battle described in the Mahabharata. On the Western calendar this took place in 3102 B.C.E. Hindus believe that when this yuga ends in chaos and with violence, Kalki the tenth avatar of Vishnu, will descend to earth to begin a new, perfect age.

Raksha Bandhan

This festival takes place on the full-moon day of the Hindu month of *Shravan* (July/August). In northern India it marks the start of the agricultural year. In western India it is a feast day and a public holiday. *Raksha* means "protection" and *Bandhan* means "to tie." On this day, Hindus tie silk thread with a bauble, as shown above, on friends' and relatives' wrists.

In many families *Raksha Bandhan* is celebrated as a sisters' day. The "tie of protection" ceremony begins with the sister putting a mark on the forehead of her brother, using *kum kum*. Then she ties the thread or *rakhi* on her brother's right wrist, saying: "May all your ambitions be fulfilled." She offers him a blessing and a milk candy, called *barfi*. He gives her a present and makes a promise to protect her throughout her life.

The *rakhi* is a symbol for protection from evil and also for the strengthening of affection between sisters and brothers. Where a girl has no brother, male cousins are regarded as brothers. The ceremony then serves also as a reminder of the importance of family unity.

Krishnajanmashtmi

This festival marks the birth of Krishna. It occurs on the eighth day of the dark half of *Shravan*. People fast until midnight. In homes and temples, they read from the scriptures and sing devotional songs. They adorn *murtis* of Krishna and his companion, Radha, and place gifts of milk candies, fruit, leaves, and flowers at their feet.

At the festival to mark the birth of Krishna, a cradle holding an image of Krishna as a baby is displayed in mandirs. *Parents bring their children to this* murti *to be blessed by Krishna.*

At midnight, *puja* and *arti* ceremonies are performed. The fast is broken by sharing the food, or *prashad*, blessed by God. Often a *murti* of Krishna as a baby in a cradle is revealed at midnight, and parents bring their children to the *murti* to be blessed.

Mahasivratri

Mahashivratri means the "Great Night of Siva." Many Hindus will fast every Monday as a mark of devotion to Siva. On *Mahasivratri*, on the fourteenth day of the dark fortnight of *Magha* (January/February), the whole family may fast. Many families do not eat cooked meals but only fruit, nuts, and *barfi*.

Navratri, Durgapuja, *and* Dassehra

Navratri, which means "nine nights," occurs after the monsoon rains, during the first ten days of the light half of the month of *Ashvina* (September/October). One of the few Hindu festivals celebrated all over India, it is also popular in the West. In India it has different names in different places. It is called *Navratri* in Gujarat in western India, *Durgapuja* in Bengal in eastern India, and *Dassehra* in northern India. Some of the celebrations differ, too.

In Gujarat, India, and in the West, the festival of Navratri *is marked by traditional dancing for nine nights.*

Navratri is an important Gujarati Hindu festival that is dedicated to the worship of the mother goddess, in one or many of her forms. Ambaji is one of her names. A general term, *mataji*, meaning "honored mother," is also used.

The celebrations include dancing around a special shrine made from a box with a cone-shaped top. There is a picture of the mother goddess in one of her forms on each side. There are two traditional dances: *garba*, a circle dance, and *dandya ras*, a stick dance. The dancing and devotional singing begin in the evening and continue well into the night. Hindus of all ages attend, some for the whole period of nine nights. It is a time for renewing friendships and strengthening community bonds.

FASTING

Men, women, and older children fast during some festivals and at other times. Women may fast on a regular basis, as part of their duties. Some, on the eleventh day of each fortnight, will have only one meal. This regular fast is called *agiaras*.

Many Hindus regard *Shravan* as a holy month. In this month, they eat only once a day, usually after sunset. Brahmin families in particular fast on Mondays of this month and break their fast after sunset. Devout Hindus avoid spicy foods and alcohol. Many men, mostly from Brahmin families, do not shave during *Shravan*. In these ways Hindus practice self-discipline, learn to control desires, and show devotion to God.

The nights are noisy, bright with colorful clothes and decorations, and full of energy. The goddess represents Shakti, or energy and power. Hindus believe that the goddess's energy lives in them. They awaken it by taking part in the festival, and it can then be used to overcome the evil that they meet in daily life. At the end of each night, the *arti* ceremony is performed and *prashad* is shared.

The goddess Durga is worshiped at the festival of *Durgapuja* in Bengal. This also lasts for nine nights. On the tenth day the festival murtis of Durga are carried to the river and immersed in the water. This is a way of saying that it is not the image that is important, but the deity herself. Another meaning is that the water carries away the bad things of life.

Diwali

Diwali is the most important Hindu festival and the main one celebrated in the West. The word is a shortened version of *Deepavali*, which means "a row of lights." The festival differs from place to place, but in most cases people clean their homes and decorate them with garlands of flowers and paper chains. They light oil lamps. They wear new clothes and feast with relatives and friends.

The message of *Diwali* is that good overcomes evil and light can triumph over darkness. For many Hindus,

THE STORY OF RAMA AND SITA

Prince Rama and his wife Sita lived in the kingdom of Ayodhya in India. Through no fault of his, Rama was denied his place on the throne when his father, the king, died. He was banished to a forest for 14 years, with Sita and his half-brother, Lakshmana. In the forest, Sita was captured by the king of demons, Ravana. He imprisoned her on the island of Lanka (now Sri Lanka).

After many battles and much struggle, Rama, helped by the forest animals and especially the monkey deity Hanuman, defeated Ravana and rescued Sita. Rama and Sita returned to Ayodhya, where Rama became king. For many Hindus, *Diwali* celebrates this return.

On the third day of Diwali *Hindu business people close their account books and offer worship to Lakshmi, praying for prosperity. In the West this ceremony is often held in a* mandir, *which gets very crowded.*

Diwali celebrates the story of Rama and Sita and their return to their kingdom in India. Other stories linked with the festival are a tale of how Krishna defeated a demon called Naraka and a story of King Bali's generous spirit.

Another part of *Diwali* is the worship of the goddess Lakshmi, who represents wealth as well as grace. On the third day, the house and surrounding areas are lit with oil lamps. Especially in Indian villages, people keep their doors and windows open. This is an invitation to Lakshmi to enter and bless the household.

The fourth day of the festival is considered the most auspicious. A married woman receives a present from her husband, and children wear new clothes. It is a day for new beginnings, and it resembles the marking of a New Year in other world customs.

Diwali *is also a time for exchanging and sharing sweet food.*

Glossary

To show how words are pronounced, some stress marks have been added to the words in this Glossary.

a sounds like the <u>a</u> in "human."
ā sounds like the <u>a</u> in "car."
i sounds like the <u>i</u> in "sit."
ī sounds like the <u>ee</u> in "meet."
u sounds like the <u>u</u> in "bull."
ū sounds like the <u>oo</u> in "soon."

agiaras	The eleventh day of each half of the lunar month, when many Hindus fast. Used mostly by Gujarati Hindus.
ahimsā	Not killing; nonviolence – linked with respect for all forms of life.
ārti	An act of worship in which a cotton wick or wicks, dipped in clarified butter, are lit in front of an image of a deity and moved in a circle to show reverence.
ātman	Self or soul in individuals; a spark of God in humans.
avatār	"Descent to earth"; an incarnation of God on earth, come to destroy evil.
bhajan	Devotional song or hymn, sometimes chanted to music.
bhakti	Devotion to God.
Brahmin	Member of a priestly group, the first of the four varnas.
chakra	Wheel with 32 spokes. It has been adopted as India's national symbol.
dharma	Duty or conduct, right living, correct actions, or religion.
dīvā	A twisted cotton wick dipped in clarified butter and placed in a lamp made of earthenware or brass.
fast	A type of self-sacrifice which can mean not eating or drinking at all; or drinking only water and milk; or eating only certain foods, such as fruits.
ghee	Melted clarified butter.
gurū	A religious teacher or guide, who helps to remove ignorance in the world.
homa	A fire ritual, mainly performed at weddings, during which offerings of wood, ghee, and grains are made to the god of fire, Agni.
jāti	The social group, or caste, to which a Hindu belongs by birth. Usually linked to an occupation.
karma	The belief that all actions have effects, good and bad. A person's actions determine his or her future in this life and the next.
kathā	A gathering at which religious stories are told and explained by a priest.
kum kum	A red or saffron-colored powder, made into a paste and used to anoint a deity.
mala	A string of 108 beads, usually made from wood, used for prayer.
mandir	A Hindu temple or shrine.
mantra	A sacred syllable, word, or prayer, usually repeated when recited.

46

moksha	Final freedom from the cycle of birth, death, and rebirth.
murti	Image of a deity, used as a focus for worship.
om	The sacred sound representing God, the Supreme Being.
pandit	A learned man, usually a Brahmin.
prashād	Food such as fruit, nuts, and sweets that is offered to deities and shared by Hindus after worship.
pūjā	An act of worship performed at home at the family shrine or in a mandir.
pūjāri	A brahmin who conducts *puja* in a *mandir* and advises families in religious matters.
samsāra	Life in the world as a cycle of birth, death, and rebirth.
samskār	Sacrament; life-cycle ritual.
Sanātan dharma	"Eternal" or "ageless" religion; a term used by Hindus for "Hinduism."
satsang	A gathering for devotional singing and worship.
shruti	"That which is heard;" scriptures "revealed" by God.
smriti	"That which is remembered;" scriptures based on traditions.
tilak	A mark made of *kum kum* and put on a worshiper's forehead. It is a sign of respect and blessing.
varna	Literally "color." Ancient Hindu society was divided into four varnas – groups.

Book List

Denny, Roz. *A Taste of India.* Food Around the World. New York: Thomson Learning, 1994.

Ganeri, Anita. *Benares.* Holy Cities. New York: Macmillan, 1993.

Ganeri, Anita. *The Indian Subcontinent.* Places and People. New York: Franklin Watts, 1994.

Gordon, Susan. *Asian Indians.* Recent American Immigrants. New York: Franklin Watts, 1990.

Mitter, S. *Hindu Festivals.* Holidays and Festivals. Vero Beach, FL: Rourke, 1989.

Srinivasan, A. V. *Hindu Primer: Yaksha Prashna.* Glastonbury, CT: Ind-US, 1984.

Wangu, Madhu Bazaz. *Hinduism.* World Religions. New York: Facts on File, 1991.

Warner, Rachel. *Indian Migrations.* Migrations. New York: Thomson Learning, 1995.

Note on Dates

Each religion has its own system for counting the years of its history. The starting point may be related to the birth or death of a special person or an important event. In everyday life, today, when different communities have dealings with each other, they use the same counting system for setting dates in the future and writing accounts of the past. The Western system is now used throughout the world. It is based on Christian beliefs about Jesus: A.D. (Anno Domini = in the year of our Lord) and B.C. (Before Christ). Members of the various world faiths use the common Western system, but, instead of A.D. and B.C., they say and write C.E. (in the Common Era) and B.C.E. (before the Common Era).

Index